Foreword

THE THREE-YEAR GARDEN RECORDKEEPER is the essential gardener's diary, perfect for recording the weekly, seasonal, and yearly changes that make each garden unique.

Each month THE THREE-YEAR GARDEN RECORDKEEPER features a description of a garden style with appropriate plant suggestions, to help you dream about, plan, or revise your garden design. In addition, there are seasonal reminders, lists of garden chores, ideas for garden-related crafts, and tips on garden design and maintenance, plus a handy climate zone chart for your easy reference. THE THREE-YEAR GARDEN RECORDKEEPER is designed to hold all your garden-related thoughts. Use the ample space provided each week to record all the activity in your garden, comment on the progress of plantings, make yearly comparisons, jot down new ideas, note unusual events, or just write down your impressions. THE THREE-YEAR GARDEN RECORDKEEPER allows you to record the life of your garden and thereby enhance your gardening experience.

Garden Planning

THE MOST IMPORTANT CONSIDERATION WHEN planning a garden is not style, nor plant material, nor even soil conditions, but rather, how the garden is going to be used. Before making any decisions about the type of garden you want, ask yourself the following questions. Your answers will help you to create a garden that will give you pleasure for seasons to come.

- Who will be using the garden?
- What are your family needs? Will children play in the garden? Do you want to create a separate play area?
- Will you entertain in the garden? Is a barbecue necessary? Should there be a spot for dining? A patio?
- Will the garden be the center of outdoor sports? Would a badminton area, basketball hoop, or tennis court be practical?
- Do you want fruits, vegetables, or herbs from your garden? Will you want easy access from the kitchen?
- Is your garden to be a source of cut flowers? Perhaps a separate cutting garden would be a good idea?
- Will you use the garden at night?
- Is fragrance important to you?
- How much privacy do you want?
- How much time do you want to devote to maintenance?
- Do you want to use the garden in all four seasons?

Much time, effort, and confusion can be saved by intelligently planning the garden and deciding what your needs are before buying and planting.

January 1 – January 7

YEAR 1

YEAR 2

YEAR 3

Garden Design

THE BASIC ELEMENTS OF ANY GARDEN DESIGN ARE scale, composition, perspective, color, texture, and shape.

Scale may be defined as how one part of the design relates to another. With proper scale, the size and relationship of each element to the other is proportionate—no one part of the garden is allowed to dominate—unless you want it to. Scale also concerns how the garden relates to the environment around it.

Composition refers to the organization of the elements within the garden—plants, ornaments, number of colors, containers, and so on. The object is to create a pleasing balance, with movement and rhythm, but without crowding or busyness.

Perspective in garden design deals with the spatial relationships within the garden—how the elements work together to draw the eye around the garden.

Color lends the garden its emotional tone and creates eye-catching focal points. Using color pleasingly is more difficult than one might expect—beginners should stick to fast-blooming annuals, so that unpleasing schemes can be changed easily.

Shape comes from the trees and shrubs that are used in the garden to add decorative effects.

Texture is created by using plants with differing leaf forms and branching to avoid uniformity and add depth.

January 8 - January 14

YEAR 1

YEAR 2

YEAR 3

Catalogue Ordering

In January, gardeners' mailboxes are suddenly clogged with colorful catalogues from nurseries around the country. Most gardeners anticipate this time of year with glee, although selecting the best plants for your garden from among so many choices can be daunting. Yet if you use some forethought, investing money in mail-order plants can pay off handsomely. Before you sit down to look at the catalogues, know your garden's conditions in detail—the sheltered cold spots; wet, soggy areas; dry clay soils; and so on. This will aid in choosing plants that will survive season after season in your garden's specific microclimate.

Before you buy, draw up a pencil plan of your garden, marking the basic trees, shrubs, and large plantings. Label important flowering plants with color felt-tip pens. This is your existing site blueprint, which you can use to plan out where to put additions from your catalogue collections, or to redesign your garden for the coming season.

January 15 – January 21

YEAR 1

YEAR 2

YEAR 3

Your Garden Blueprint

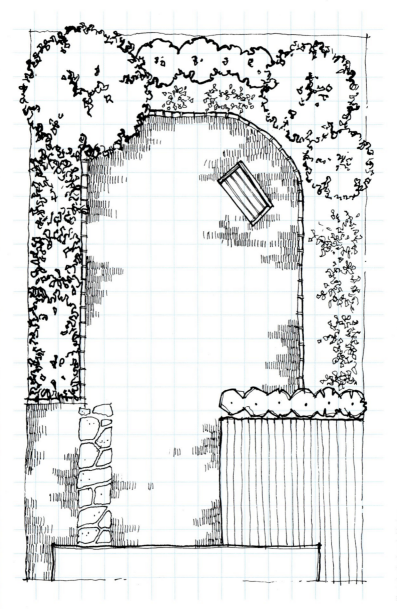

A typical garden blueprint—try drawing your own.

January 22 – January 28

YEAR 1

YEAR 2

YEAR 3

Rock Gardens

Rocks in a garden may be viewed as obstacles or they may represent the opportunity to create your own alpine hill. Fortunate is the gardener with a hilly slope, rock outcropping, stone ledge, or gravel scree on which to grow alpine plants.

Three basic elements must be considered in the design of your rock garden: the rocky site, rock placement, and plant material. If your site is not natural for a rock garden, consider arranging nature slightly to accommodate one. You can make a stone outcropping by partially embedding large rocks in the soil. Form an L shape by placing the largest rock in one corner and following with smaller rocks to complete the angle. Fill the space with scree soil mixture: Mix two parts stone chips, one part leaf mold, and one part soil to use all through the garden plot. To keep the area free of weeds and insure air circulation between plants and soil, spread yellowstone mulch between the plants.

Alpine plants are suitable for all rock gardens. In warmer climates, succulents and small cacti make excellent rock garden plants as well.

Rock Garden Favorites

Alchemilla vulgaris	Lady's Mantle
Aquilegia alpina	Columbine
Aster alpinus	Rock Aster
Dianthus alpinus	Alpine Pink
Galium odoratum	Sweet Woodruff
Houstonia caerulea	Bluet
Iberis sempervirens	Evergreen Candytuft
Papaver alpinum	Alpine Poppy
Phlox subulata	Moss Pink
Primula auricula	Primrose
Sanguinaria canadensis	Bloodroot
Sedum sieboldii	Stonecrop

January 29 – February 4

YEAR 1

YEAR 2

YEAR 3

Rock garden featuring alpine plants.

February 5 – February 11

YEAR 1

YEAR 2

YEAR 3

Cold Frames

A COLD FRAME IS A WOODEN, BOXLIKE STRUCTURE with a glass or plastic lid, under which sunlight is trapped, thereby heating up the air within the frame. The cold frame allows you to grow plants in the ground even in cold climates, protected from inclement weather and incubated by heated surface soil. As in a green house, the temperature and moisture buildup can be regulated by propping open the lid.

You can build a cold frame to any specifications. There are many kits available through mail-order catalogues and from garden supply stores.

In early spring, use the cold frame to start seedlings. The sun should keep the temperature inside around 70–75°F (21–24°C). Open the lid if it gets much higher. If there's a late spring frost, an old blanket over the cold frame will prevent the temperature from dropping too low.

Start vegetables early in the cold frame, and have a spring harvest of lettuce, spinach, and radishes. The cold frame can also extend the growing season into fall and act as a storage cellar in winter for vegetables that are best kept very cold, such as root vegetables.

February 12 - February 18

YEAR 1

YEAR 2

YEAR 3

Forcing Bulbs

Even in winter you can have daffodils blooming in your kitchen, if you know how to force bulbs. Forcing garden variety daffodils, tulips, crocii, and hyacinths is easy if you have some planting pots and extra room in your refrigerator.

Use a clay pot that is at least twice as tall as the bulbs. Place a piece of newspaper over the hole, and fill the pot with a soil mixture of peat and sand. Place the bulbs in the pot with the growing tips pointing upward. Cover them with soil, allowing the tips to peek out slightly. Water thoroughly and label each pot with the date and variety of each bulb. Place them in an unheated basement, garage, cold frame, or in the refrigerator.

After about eight weeks in cold storage, the roots and stems should begin to bulge out. Put them in a sunny spot and wait for buds to form. Soon you will have an early spring bloom.

Many spring shrubs will also open their buds indoors. Cut branches of forsythia, for example, on a warm day, and smash or slit the ends of the branches. This will enable water to be absorbed up the branch to pop the buds open. Strip bark from the lower area of the branches before plunging them into warm water.

February 19 – February 25

YEAR 1

YEAR 2

YEAR 3

Tree Pruning

An arborist studies trees and shrubs and performs cultivation, maintenance, and professional pruning. For major tree maintenance, which can be dangerous work, always call a specialist. Minor tree pruning, however, you can do yourself.

Why prune trees? To remove dead and diseased limbs and to increase natural strength; to remove suckers and "water" sprouts that rob the tree's energy for flowering and fruiting; to clear limbs from walkways and views, and to distance heavy foliage from the house. Pruning also helps improve the appearance of the trees.

The best time to prune is in late winter or early spring, before new growth begins. Light design pruning can be done in early spring or summer when the tree is fully leafed out, but major pruning should be done when your trees are dormant.

Trees heal their wounds by making a scablike growth. Gardeners can aid the healing process by making a proper "bandage." Clean away dead bark with a sharp knife, and do not gouge the tree. Wrap plastic around the wound and use black electrical tape to secure it in place. Leave the bandage on for one year, taking care that sunlight does not shine through. The tree will take care of the rest.

February 26 – March 4

YEAR 1

YEAR 2

YEAR 3

Topiary

TOPIARY IS A GARDEN ART FORM DEVELOPED BY THE ancient Romans. Simply defined, topiary is the art of shaping plants into specific forms, and is achieved by careful pruning and clipping.

Many plants can be trained into standard forms. You can prune existing hedges, mass plantings, or accent plants. A small boxwood hedge grown as a perimeter to enclose a perennial border makes a lovely formal accent. If you have an evergreen at the entrance of your house, consider clipping it in a spiral form. A globe or ball atop a tree or shrub having one main bare stem is a form that is also attractive in a container. When you decide to incorporate shapes into a present garden design, be careful not to distort every existing shrub so that all of your natural growth forms disappear. Topiary should stand out as a unique example of formal gardening.

Mock topiary, which speeds up the process by two to three years, develops a green plant on a wire frame. Kits can be ordered from a catalogue, or you can make wire shapes yourself.

Topiary Shrubs
Boxwood
Hemlock
Holly
Juniper
Privet
Yew

Mock Frame Topiary
Creeping Fig
English Ivy
Winter Creeper

March 5 – March 11

YEAR 1

YEAR 2

YEAR 3

Garden Ornaments and Furniture

GARDEN ORNAMENTS ARE THE DECORATIVE accessories in garden design. Each garden has individual objects that distinguish one style from another. In Japanese gardens, you will find stone lanterns, bamboo fences, buddha statues, and granite basins. A Victorian garden may contain a wooden bench, a gazebo, a hothouse, or a conservatory. A functional sundial or pedestal can act as focal point in a dooryard garden. A fragrance garden might have an arbor of old roses. A night garden will feature carefully hidden path-lights to show the way without outshining the stars. A wildlife garden must contain a bird bath, house, and feeder. Stone rabbits, frogs, and turtles hide in a children's garden. Pots, vases, and sculptures enliven quiet corners. Fountains bring the calming sound of cool running water.

No matter how lovely your trees, shrubs, perennials, and other plants are, a garden is always enhanced by ornamental statuary, benches, fences, and other accessories. And once the period of bloom has died down, your garden ornaments will play a stronger role, so choose carefully.

March 12 – March 18

YEAR 1

YEAR 2

YEAR 3

Flower Shows

MARCH IS THE MONTH WHEN LOCAL FLOWER shows are generally held. Most flower shows feature design displays, flower exhibits, lectures by gardening experts, demonstrations by suppliers, contests, and other attractions.

Thematic displays may range from reconstructed Victorian gardens to futuristic garden visions. The plants in most of these displays will be labelled with their proper botanical names, so bring a pad and pen for note taking.

Contests are another common feature of flower shows. Competitions may be held in flower arranging, topiary, or growing outstanding specimens of such plants as African violets or orchids.

The marketplace at most flower shows is not to be missed. Vendors set up mini stores to sell supplies, tools and equipment, and plants.

Your local nursery or gardening association can give you information on the dates and locations of regional flower shows. You might also consider visiting flower shows while on vacation—the local tourism office can direct you.

March 19 – March 25

YEAR 1

YEAR 2

YEAR 3

Shade Gardens

IF YOUR GARDEN AREA DOES NOT RECEIVE DIRECT sunlight, do not despair—design a shade garden. Whether the shade is caused by heavy tree growth or by the shadows of city towers, you can create a garden that will thrive in your particular microclimate.

A shade garden's advantage is coolness. Summer heat does not easily penetrate a canopy of trees or a wall of highrises. The shade garden can be a cool, green oasis, a fragrant retreat from the hot sun, where shade-loving flowers will flourish. Most shady sites have moist soil climates, in which native wildflowers, such as the primrose, are quite content.

The well-designed shade garden utilizes all the available sun spaces. It incorporates garden features and uses color combinations to create a garden in which certain light spots will catch the eye and pull it away from dark corners. To begin, thin the foliage of large shade trees by pruning from the inside out to allow more sunlight to enter the garden. White flowers and leaves will stand out against a dark background. Use pinks, violets, and plants with white-veined leaves as focal points, and as specimen plants in corners of the shade garden.

March 26 - April 1

YEAR 1

YEAR 2

YEAR 3

Shade-Garden Plants

White Bloomers
(Common names)
Astilbe
Begonia
Cleome
Cyclamen
Goatsbeard
Impatiens
Japanese Anemone
Solomon's Seal

Bulbs
Caladium
Daffodil
English Ivy
Hosta
Scilla
Snowdrop
Wild Ginger
Winter Aconite

Shade Lovers
Bluebell
Columbine
Dicentra
Foam Flower
Forget-me-not
Primrose
Phlox
Rhododendron
Spiderwort
Veronica

April 2 – April 8

YEAR 1

YEAR 2

YEAR 3

Spring Garden Chores

IN NORTHERN CLIMATES, GARDENS TRULY SPRING TO life in April and gardeners must spring into action. A list of chores commonly undertaken at this time of year may be helpful.

- Lawn care begins; reseed on a rainy day. Fertilize.
- Start herb seeds for planting indoors.
- Do not mow down bulb foliage yet.
- When it is dry enough, work the soil in flowerbeds and vegetable areas. Test and fertilize if necessary.
- Take a look at your compost pile. Turn it over to increase the decay process. Use bottom compost to turn into planting beds.
- Rose care begins; remove any protective winter coverings. Heavy winter mulches can be removed. Spray with mildew preventative, fertilize, set stakes, repair trellis.
- Zones 8–10, put out house plants and water well.
- Fertilize house plants; spray for pests.
- Check water gardens for winter damage.
- Move cool-weather vegetables to cold frames.
- Feed and prune fruit trees.
- Prune spring-flowering shrubs after they bloom.
- Plant tomatoes and stake for upward growth.
- Plant field-grown evergreens; remember to work peat moss into holes before planting. Water thoroughly between rainfalls.
- Compare local spring sales for the best pick of the early annuals, perennials, and flowering hanging pots.

April 9 – April 15

YEAR 1

YEAR 2

YEAR 3

Bulbs

BULBS FIT INTO ANY GARDEN DESIGN. THEY MAKE A grand statement planted alone and add color when mixed into rock gardens or perennial beds. Suitable for water gardens, small city spaces, and containers, bulbs add striking effect year-round.

April 16 - April 22

YEAR 1

YEAR 2

YEAR 3

Year-Round Blooming Bulbs

January	Zones 8–10	Aconite; Daffodil
February	Zones 4–7	Snowdrop
March	Zones 4–7	Chionodoxa; Scilla; Crocus; Dwarf Iris
April **May**	All Zones	Allium; Anemone; Calla Lily; Canna; Daffodil; Fritillaria; Grape Hyancinth; Lily of the Valley; Ranuncula; Species Tulips; Tuberous Begonia
June **July** **August**	All Zones	Daylilies; Galtonia; Gladiolus; Agapanthus; Tuberous Begonias; Cannas; Caladium; Eremurus
September **October**	All Zones	Colchicum; Autumn Crocus; Hardy Cyclamen
November **December**	Indoors	Freesia; Amaryllis; Paperwhite Narcissus

April 23 – April 29

YEAR 1

YEAR 2

YEAR 3

Water Gardens

THE IDEAL GARDEN SITE FOR GROWING WATER-loving plants features a stream or a small pond. If nature has not so provided, consider a man-made addition. Water gardens are generally very easy to maintain. Water-loving plants are prolific growers and provide both height and dense fullness in one season. Moisture is ever present, weeds are choked out, and less pruning is required. Water plants do have very specific water requirements, however, so be sure to check the needs of your proposed plants before planting.

Water-Loving Plants

Caltha palustrus	Marsh Marigold
Cyperus alternifolius	Umbrella Plant
Iris pseudacorus	Yellow Flag Iris
Lythrum salicaria	Purple Loosestrife
Myosotis scorpiodes	Water Forget-me-nots
Pontederia cordata	Pickerelweed
Typha latifolia	Cattails
Zantedeschia aethiopica	Calla Lily

April 30 – May 6

YEAR 1

YEAR 2

YEAR 3

Shrubs

Shrubs are the main structures around which all other plant material is designed. Shrubs add texture, color, shape, and dimension. They can be used to fill in the spaces between house and garden, create garden rooms, and provide privacy.

Shrubs have practical uses, too: Thorny shrubs can be used for traffic control, evergreen shrubs for barriers and noise mufflers, fruit-bearing shrubs for wildlife food, and fragrant flower shrubs for scenting the garden.

Flowering Shrubs
Abelia grandiflora (Glossy Abelia)
Chionanthus virginicus (Fringe Tree)
Lonicera (Honeysuckle)
Magnolia stellata (Star Magnolia)
Rhododendron
Rosa rugosa (Rugosa Rose)
Viburnum

Fruiting Shrubs
Cornus mas (Cornelian Cherry)
Cotoneaster dammeri (Bearberry Cotoneaster)
Ilex cornuta (Chinese Holly)
Lonicera fragrantissima (Winter Honeysuckle)
Rosa helenae (Helen Rose)
Taxus cuspidata (Japanese Yew)

Winter Foliage
Cotoneaster horizontalis (Rock Spray)
Euonymus fortunei (Wintercreeper)
Ilex crenata (Japanese Holly)
Rhododendron fortunei (Fortune Rhododendron)
Viburnum japonicum (Japanese Viburnum)

May 7 – May 13

YEAR 1

YEAR 2

YEAR 3

Planting Shrubs

SHRUBS ARE SOLD IN THREE BASIC FORMS: BARE-rooted, balled and burlapped, and container-grown. Basic planting instructions:

- dig a hole at least twice as large as the root ball
- remove six inches of topsoil and put aside
- take out six inches of subsoil and discard
- mix organic matter, peat moss, and fertilizer into topsoil
- fill bottom half of hole with augmented soil
- water deeply and frequently, and protect from wind and cold

    You have now created an environment for the shrub's root system to spread out, gather nutrients, and grow vigorously, rewarding you with a spectacular burst of color each season.

    Never allow *bare-rooted* shrubs to dry out. Submerge the roots in a tub of muddy water (topsoil added) until you are ready to plant. Shear off any damaged or broken roots and branches. *Balled and burlapped* shrubs can be planted as is. Just be sure to cut and loosen the burlap and bury it below the soil line. *Container-grown* shrubs are invariably pot-bound. The medium is usually a soil-free mixture of peat, bark, and perlite, in which the plant can die of strangulation and drought. Remove the container and examine the root system. Pry as many roots as free as possible and prune off any roots too close to the crown. Loosen the soil around the base to encourage the root system to grow outward. Prune the top third of growth to compensate for the roots removed.

May 14 - May 20

YEAR 1

YEAR 2

YEAR 3

Viburnum plicatum 'mariesii'.

May 21 – May 27

YEAR 1

YEAR 2

YEAR 3

Window Boxes

ANNUAL-FILLED WINDOW BOXES ARE EASY TO CARE for—all they need is water, water, water. The right spot is anywhere support is available, from urban terraces and patios to fences, benches, and, of course, window ledges.

Annual combinations

- Salmon geranium, dusty miller, white alyssum
- English ivy, lavender, purple pansy
- Morning glory and sweet pea
- Basil, mint, marigold
- Begonia all alone
- Fiery red salvia, geranium, celosia
- Blue browallia, deep indigo lobelia, ivy
- Orange and yellow nasturtium, zinnia, pansy
- California poppy, nasturtium
- Portulaca, echeveria succulent
- Vinca periwinkle, vinca vine, impatiens

May 28 – June 3

YEAR 1

YEAR 2

YEAR 3

The Lure of Fragrance

WHEN DESIGNING ANY GARDEN, PLAN TO LOCATE A few fragrant plants near seating areas to further enhance the sensory appeal of your garden. Use this list to select the most fragrant plants.

Latin name	Common Name	Scent
Datura species	Angel's Trumpet*	Heavy musk
Centaurea	Bachelor's Button	Light and airy
Rosmarinus officinalis	Creeping Rosemary*	Herbaceous
Nicotiana alata	Flowering Tobacco	Sweet
Freesia x *kewensis*	Freesia*	Sweet
Gardenia jasminoide	Gardenia	Sweet and heavy
Pelargonium	Geranium (scented)*	Lemon or rose
Jasminum species	Jasmine	Springtime perfume
Lavendula species	Lavender	Sweet and heavy
Citrus species	Orange and Lemon trees	Citrus
Calendula	Pot Marigold	Earthy
Rosa varieties	Rose*	Sweet
Stephanotis floribunda	Stephanotis	Fresh and flowering
Wisteria sinensis	Wisteria	Light and sweet

*Night-fragrance plants

June 4 – June 10

YEAR 1

YEAR 2

YEAR 3

Secret Garden

"It's a secret garden,
and I'm the only one in the world
who wants it to be alive."
Frances Hodgson Burnett
The Secret Garden, 1938

A SECRET GARDEN IS A SPOT THAT IS SECLUDED, EVEN hidden, a place where the imagination roams free. The secret garden can be a child's hideaway, a lover's rendezvous, a place of one's own, or a secluded retreat.

You can make your own concealed garden using the features of your present site. A hedge can hide a secret spot from view. A path through shady trees can open onto a quiet clearing, perhaps with a round table and two wrought-iron chairs for secluded dining. An arbor or trellis filled with dangling bunches of wisteria, fragrant climbing roses, or hardy clematis will make a superb entryway.

Plants to Include in a Secret Garden

Allium neapolitanum 'Grandiflorum'	Naples Onion
Astilbe x *arendsii*	Hybrid Astilbe
Begonia x *tuberhybrida*	Tuberous Begonia
Cleome	Spiderflower
Impatiens	Snapweed
Lilium	Lily
Paeonia	Peony
Phlox carolina	Carolina Phlox

June 11 - June 17

YEAR 1

YEAR 2

YEAR 3

Potpourri

POTPOURRI IS A FRAGRANT MIXTURE OF DRIED flowers, spices, leaves, and natural plant oils. Each recipe is unique and creates a special perfume. You can easily make your own potpourri from ingredients in your garden and kitchen.

Flowers	Botanicals	Leaves/Fillers
Chamomile	Cinnamon sticks	Guassia chips
Hibiscus	Cloves	Lemon verbena leaves
Lavender	Ground nutmeg	Patchouli leaves
Marigold	Orange peel	Powdered orris root
Old Rose		Safflower
Tuberose		Scented geranium

Many scent shops sell these ingredients if you don't wish to harvest your own.

The moist potpourri method is the easiest way to make your own blend. Take freshly picked flowers and layer them sandwich style with sea salt (non-iodized) in a closed container. Put a heavy rock atop this mixture to press out all of the moisture. Open the container regularly and stir the mixture about, adding more alternate layers of salt and flowers. When ready to use, transfer the mixture to an open bowl and add any blend of spices that you fancy. The result is a wonderful, personalized potpourri.

June 18 – June 24

YEAR 1

YEAR 2

YEAR 3

Perennial Borders

PERENNIALS ARE HERBACEOUS PLANTS (NO WOODY tissue) whose leafy forms die back each winter while their resilient root stocks lie dormant under the soil. Come spring or summer, they bloom again. Perennials will provide stunning color in your garden.

Designing with perennials often means creating perennial borders, which are beds filled with these colorful plants used as drifts or along edges.

Perennial borders can be created in any space, width, or length. You can mix differently textured and shaped plants together, including spike flowers, mound flowers, bushy forms, and leafy plants.

When planning color schemes, keep in mind that graduated colors are often more pleasing to the eye than contrasting or clashing shades. An example is a bed of white flowers graduating to pinks, fuchsias, and violets, then to deep purples and blues. Contrasting colors, such as purple and yellow, can be striking together, but such combinations are more difficult to design well. When you choose your plants, you are really painting a picture. You may find it helpful to plan it out beforehand, sketching your proposed site and filling in your potential perennial beds with colored pencils. Perennial borders will soften the edges of paths or walls, and drifts planted in the middle of a lawn will relieve the green with splashes of color, while adding structural interest to your garden.

Jot down your impressions of your perennial beds in each season. Note the colors that clash, heights that look out of place, and any pest problems. Note also the most pleasing elements of your design. Each year discard or add plants to achieve your desired garden style. Feel free to move plants about the flower bed until you're satisfied with your composition.

June 25 – July 1

YEAR 1

YEAR 2

YEAR 3

A perennial border.

July 2 – July 8

YEAR 1

YEAR 2

YEAR 3

Perennials

VERSATILE PERENNIALS—ONE FOR EVERY gardener's plot—number in the hundreds. Perennials come in every color and there are varieties suited to every microclimate.

A Perennial Sampler

Low Perennials
Alchemilla (Lady's Mantle)
Artemisia (Silver Mound)
Campanula (Bells)
Dianthus (Carnations)
Hosta (Plantain Lily)
Primula (Primrose)

Yellow
Achillea (Yarrow)
Anthemis (Marguerite)
Caltha (Marsh Marigold)
Coreopsis (Calliopsis)
Hellebores (Christmas Rose)
Rudbeckia (Black-eyed Susan)
Solidago (Goldenrod)

Whites
Aquilegia (Columbine)
Aster
Papaver (Poppy)
Phlox
Veronica (Speedwell)

Larger Perennials
Aruncus (Goatsbeard)
Hibiscus (Rosemallow)
Miscanthus (Pampas Grass)
Thalictrum (Meadowrue)

Red
Astilbe
Chrysanthemum
Hibiscus (Rose Mallow)
Lobelia (Cardinal Flower)
Monarda (Bee Balm)
Primula (Primrose)
Sedum

Blue
Baptisia (False Indigo)
Campanula (Harebell)
Delphinium
Echinops (Globe Thistle)
Lupinus (Lupine)
Lythrum (Loosestrife)
Veronica (Speedwell)

July 9 - July 15

YEAR 1

YEAR 2

YEAR 3

Perennial Maintenance

PROPER PREPARATION OF THE SOIL BED IS KEY TO ANY successful perennial growth. Double-digging is a laborious but rewarding technique of deep cultivation, in which the top layer of soil is stripped off to ten inches deep and, with another ten inches of the next sublayer, fortified with organic matter. The result is an excellent planting base for years to come.

Perennials require some maintenance. When plants are new in spring, set up stakes to support heavy plants such as delphiniums, lilies, and hollyhocks. Apply mulch to keep the soil temperature cool and weeds to a minimum.

A regular schedule of fertilizing and watering will ensure maximum flower production and winter stamina. To maintain proper flower production and size, a perennial gardener must pinch, disbud, and deadhead plants. Pinch a small amount of the perennial's growing tip to encourage sturdier growth. Disbud the plant's alternate buds to encourage top flowers to enlarge. Deadhead all spent flowers during the season to encourage new flower buds to form.

It is necessary to divide perennials to relieve overcrowding. In cold climates, divide in early spring; in warmer climates, divide in early autumn.

July 16 - July 22

YEAR 1

YEAR 2

YEAR 3

Flower Arranging

Following the basic floral arrangement principles will help define and structure your designs. When planning your arrangement, you should consider form, space, texture, and color.

Form is defined by the height, width, and geometric shape your arrangement will follow. The place you intend it for will influence your choice—a vertical triangular form, for example, would suit a mantelpiece. A table centerpiece, however, would require a low-lying form.

Space refers to the position of each flower within the arrangement. Flowers, greens, branches, and filler should complement each other, never bunching together nor gaping apart.

Texture contributes to the style of your arrangement. For example, thistles used in dry arrangements create a wild, country effect. Orchids and birds of paradise in a black lacquer vase offer sophisticated style.

Color dictates mood, emotion, and season. It brings the rest of the elements together, and will measure the success of your effort.

Begin your arrangement by inserting your filler or base. Place your strategic focal point flowers next. Fill in with less important accent flowers. Turn the arrangement around as you create, considering it from all angles, keeping in mind its balance and scale. Finally, add any finishing touches.

July 23 – July 29

YEAR 1

YEAR 2

YEAR 3

Natural Meadow Gardens

A MEADOW GARDEN IS A GRASSY PLAIN WITH various native or transplanted wildflowers growing in profusion. It may seem an impossible task to establish a meadow in a private garden, yet over the last decade wildflower gardening has grown very popular. Such gardens are low maintenance, but not no-maintenance.

What actually happens when nature is allowed to rule your garden? The strong dominant species take over, the annuals die out after one season, and you are left with black-eyed Susans and unmowed grass. You can avoid this outcome by careful design and some maintenance.

When designing your wildflower garden, concentrate on natives that are known to survive locally and species that spread easily or reseed themselves from season to season. Consult local nurseries for plant information and advice. It may take up to three years to establish your design, but be patient and do not fertilize. Your wildflowers love the native soil.

Maintenance may involve rototilling, mowing, planting plugs, and selective removal of unwanted plants.

- Rototill only if you wish to start from scratch.
- Mow at least three times a year, in late June, early September, and late November, remembering to always rake up grass so as not to smother new growth.
- Plugs are individual plants with established roots hand-planted within the meadow system.
- Each season, remove any unwanted seedlings that begin to grow, such as maples, brambles, or weeds whose seeds have blown over to your meadow area.

July 30 – August 5

YEAR 1

YEAR 2

YEAR 3

Wildflowers

Fast-Growing Wildflowers

(common names only)

Annual Baby's Breath
Black-Eyed Susan
Blue Flax
Butterfly Weed
California Poppy
Chicory
Cornflower
Cosmos
Dame's Rocket
Evening Primrose
Foxglove
Joe-Pye Weed
Lupine
Oxeye Daisy
Penstemon
Perennial Sweet Pea
Rocket Larkspur
Sunflower
Wallflower
Yarrow

August 6 – August 12

YEAR 1

YEAR 2

YEAR 3

Butterflies and Bees

WILDFLOWER GARDENS WILL ATTRACT BUTTERflies and bees. You can encourage these insects to frequent your garden by planting species that attract them. For example, the Tortoiseshell butterfly is attracted by asters, the Red Admiral butterfly by bachelor's button, the Fritillary butterfly by butterfly bush, the Edward's Hairstreak butterfly by butterfly weed, the Snout butterfly by globe amaranth and the Yellow-Tiger Swallowtail by zinnias.

Plants that Attract Bumblebees

Achillea millefolium	Yarrow
Digitalis purpurea	Foxglove
Malus species	Apple Blossoms
Mertensia virginica	Virginia Bluebells
Salvia officinalis	Sage
Sedum 'Autumn Joy'	Live Forever
Solidago canadensis	Canada Goldenrod

August 13 – August 19

YEAR 1

YEAR 2

YEAR 3

A honeybee explores a Magnolia stellata.

August 20 – August 26

YEAR 1

YEAR 2

YEAR 3

Birds

Plants that Attract Hummingbirds

(common names only)

Annual Delphinium	Nicotiana
Antirrhinum	Penstemon
Balloon Flower	Platycodon
Beardtongue	Red Cardinal Flower
Bee Balm	'Rodeo' Red
Cleome	Russell Hybrids
Larkspur	Salvia
Lobelia	Snapdragons
Lupine	Spider Flower
Monarda 'Cambridge Scarlet'	Tobacco Plant

Food that Attracts Birds

Blue Jay	Sunflower
Cardinal	Safflower seeds
Catbird	Chopped fruit
Chickadee	Sunflower hearts
Finch	Black oil sunflower
Mockingbird	Suet*
Morning Dove	Fine corn
Robin	Chopped fruit
Sparrow	Millet (white)
Woodpecker	Suet*

* beef or mutton fat

August 27 - September 2

YEAR 1

YEAR 2

YEAR 3

The Working Kitchen Garden

A WORKING KITCHEN GARDEN IS THE PRACtical gardener's ultimate achievement. There is a sense of self-sufficiency to be found in cooking meals with your own tomatoes, basil, cabbage, carrots, and so on.

Design your working garden for easy access, efficiency of space, and visual appeal. Choose a gently sloping, sunny, south-facing spot where winds tend to be calm or obstructed. Mix flowering edibles with salad greens; plant sweet peas in shades of red, pink, white, and blue side by side with snap beans and summer squash. Plant wonderful trailing nasturtiums in orange and yellow to spill over the edge of a container in which an orange tree also grows.

Remember, your design need not be strictly utilitarian. Espaliered fruit trees produce both beauty and harvest in one plant. Espalier trees grow flat against a trellis or horizontal wire supported by upright posts, often in a fan style. This method of growing fruit trees takes time and patience, but can work in the most unlikely places—from a city terrace twenty flights up to a backyard garden.

September 3 - September 9

YEAR 1

YEAR 2

YEAR 3

This herb garden features dill, tarragon, thyme, and catnip.

September 10 - September 16

YEAR 1

YEAR 2

YEAR 3

Historical Gardens

AN INTRIGUING APPROACH TO DESIGNING AN herb garden is to create a special period garden based on an historical era in which you are interested. Before you start, research your time period carefully, noting the types of plants, materials, designs, and techniques used during that era.

Some popular historical garden themes include the Biblical garden, the medieval garden, the Shakespearean garden, and the colonial garden.

Biblical gardens contain herbs mentioned in the Bible, such as anise, aloe, coriander, dill, mint, mustard, and saffron. The *medieval herb garden* generally is walled, creating a cloistered effect—a tranquil refuge. Include a fountain, and if you have a suitable tree, build a circular seat around it. The *Shakespearean garden* uses only plants mentioned by the Bard in his writings. Plays containing many herbal references include *Love's Labour's Lost*, *As You Like It*, and *Romeo and Juliet*. The *colonial garden* is formal and symmetrical, usually featuring raised beds along a central path or walkway. Herbs such as basil, borage, chamomile, comfrey, dill, fennel, licorice, parsley, and tarragon may be planted in the beds.

September 17 – September 23

YEAR 1

YEAR 2

YEAR 3

Herbal Baths

The easiest way to prepare an herbal bath is to wrap some dried herbs in a piece of cheesecloth or muslin, and hang it from the spout as you run the bathwater. Herbal baths can be refreshing or relaxing, depending on the herbs used.

Refreshing Herbs

Basil	Mint
Citronella	Rosemary
Fennel	Sage
Lavender flowers	Savory
Lemon Verbena	Thyme

Relaxing Herbs

Catnip	Mullein
Chamomile flowers	Rose flowers
Comfrey	Tansy flowers
Jasmine flowers	Valerian roots
Lemon Balm	Vervain
Linden flowers	Violet

September 24 – September 30

YEAR 1

YEAR 2

YEAR 3

The New American Garden

WHAT IS AMERICAN GARDENING? IT'S MORE relaxed, regional, seasonal, and low-maintenance. The American gardener has less time and space to produce the special garden "rooms" of formal garden design. Instead, many gardeners are using more of the plants native to their regions. Each year, these native plants survive neglect, extreme heat or cold, and other local conditions, and yet they are content in the natural soil and thrive with only the annual rainfall. Native plants thus require less maintenance because they are accustomed to the existing conditions.

One element of American gardening that is creating quite a stir is the perennial grass. Garden designers have become more interested in these previously unpopular plants. Ornamental grasses complete the three-dimensional picture in garden design, providing movement, privacy, and shelter for wildlife. They also capture sunlight.

Ornamental grasses range in size from compact mounds used for walls and ground covers to giant clumps that are used to create a focal point or specimen grouping. Their many colors include blue haze, silver streak, chartreuse, toasted almond, and white, making grasses attractive for flower arrangements and dried wreaths as well.

Cut back plants in the spring before new shoots appear. Divide them every three years with other perennials in your garden. During a drought, water deeply with soaker or dipper equipment to a six-inch (15 cm) depth. This will encourage deep roots.

October 1 - October 7

YEAR 1

YEAR 2

YEAR 3

Ornamental Grasses

Botanical Name	Common Name
Agrostis nebulosa	Cloud Bent Grass
Anthoxanthum odoratum	Sweet Vernal Grass
Avena fatua	Wild Oats
Briza maxima	Big Quaking Grass
Chasmanthium latifolium	Spike Grass
Cortaderia selloana	Pampas Grass
Elymus arenarius	European Dune Grass
Eragrostis tenella	Japanese Love Grass
Fetusca ovina glauca	Blue Fescue
Hordeum jubatum	Squirrel Tail Grass
Lamarckia aurea	Golden-top Grass
Miscanthus sinensis	Eulalia Grass
Miscanthus s. gracillimus	Maiden Grass
Miscanthus s. zebrunis	Zebra Grass
Pennisetum setaceum	Fountain Grass
Phyllostachys nigra	Black Bamboo Grass
Setaria verticillata	Bristly Foxtail Grass
Zea mays japonica	Rainbow Grass

October 8 – October 14

YEAR 1

YEAR 2

YEAR 3

Dry Soil

A UNIQUE REGION FOR GARDENING IS THE American Southwest, where plants must thrive in very dry soil conditions. Elements of this unique landscape can be brought to the home garden. Yucca and opuntia both produce species which survive colder climates. Container plants can be temporarily placed in the design, and moved indoors for protection.

Plants That Thrive in Dry Soil Conditions

Trees
Acacia minuta (Sweet Acacia)
Acer negundo (Box Elder)
Eucalyptus species (Eucalyptus)
Leptospermum laevigatum (Australian Teatree)
Prosopis glandulosa (Honey Mesquite)
Quercus virginiana (Southern Oak)

Shrubs
Artemisia species (Sagebrush)
Berberis thunbergii (Japanese Barberry)
Callistemon lanceolatus (Lemon Bottlebrush)
Hamamelis virginiana (Common Witch Hazel)
Potentilla species (Cinquefoil)
Yucca species

Perennials
Achillea (Yarrow)
Artemesia stellariana (Dusty Miller)
Baptisia australis (False Indigo)
Gypsophiia paniculata (Baby's Breath)
Lychnis coronaria (Rose Campion)
Opuntia species (Prickly Pear)
Salvia pratensis (Meadow Sage)

October 15 – October 21

YEAR 1

YEAR 2

YEAR 3

Dry–site garden.

October 22 - October 28

YEAR 1

YEAR 2

YEAR 3

Fall Clean-Up

AUTUMN IS A TIME FOR APPLE PICKING, carving Halloween pumpkins, and garden clean-up.

- In colder climates, plant spring bulbs.
- Pull on a big bulky sweater and grab a rake. Clear out fallen leaves.
- Pile squash and gourds in a wicker basket.
- Cut down bittersweet vine and fashion into a wreath.
- Poinsettias and Christmas cactus can be brought inside. The latter should have set flower buds by now.
- At the first frost, pick all green tomatoes off the vine. Place them in an open brown bag to ripen red for salads and sauce.
- In a dry autumn, water all broad-leaf evergreens and new lawn grass seed.
- Wrap plants to be protected for winter.
- Turn flower bed soil.
- Fill bird feeders.
- Prune chrysanthemums and other perennials to 5 in. (12 cm) from soil level. Remove any annuals still thriving and discard.
- Take in potted plants: herbs, geraniums, ivy.
- Dig up non-hardy bulbs such as gladiolas, dahlias, tuberoses, and store in a well-ventilated container.
- Clean and put garden tools away.

October 29 – November 4

YEAR 1

YEAR 2

YEAR 3

Autumn Color

THE DAZZLING COLORS OF AUTUMN RANGE from yellow and bronze to red and purple. As the weather grows colder, the amount of chlorophyll normally produced by leaves is gradually reduced, until little or none is manufactured. At this stage, leaves turn yellow, for the yellow pigments that are usually masked by chlorophyll now become dominant.

The outstanding reds of autumn are the work of another pigment, which results from the accumulation of sugars and tannins in the leaves. Brilliant autumn reds require warm, sunny days followed by cool nights.

All leaves eventually turn brown, as the leaf tissue fully decays. Before that happens, take a walk through the woods and collect some colorful examples to take home and use for fall arrangements or crafts.

November 5 - November 11

YEAR 1

YEAR 2

YEAR 3

Trees for Autumn Color

Yellow
Acer pensylvanicum (Striped Maple)
Acer saccharinum (Silver Maple)
Betula species (Birches)
Hamamelis mollis (Chinese Witch Hazel)
Populus alba (White Poplar)

Bronze
Carya species (Hickory)
Castanea dentata (American Chestnut)
Fagus grandifolia (American Beech)
Magnolia stellata (Star Magnolia)

Red
Acer rubrum (Red Maple)
Acer saccharum (Sugar Maple)
Cornus alba siberica (Siberian Dogwood)
Quercus rubra (Red Oak)
Quercus coccinea (Scarlet Oak)
Rhus aromatica (Fragrant Sumac)

Red-Purple
Fraxinus americana (White Ash)
Gaultheria procumbens (Wintergreen)
Juniperus virginiana (Eastern Red Cedar)
Quercus alba (White Oak)
Viburnum lentago (Nannyberry)

November 12 – November 18

YEAR 1

YEAR 2

YEAR 3

Gardener's Gift Catalogues

A GREAT METHOD OF SHOPPING FOR GARDENing gifts (at any time of year) is through the vast array of mail-order catalogues available. Regular browsing will also keep you up to date on new garden products, books, seeds, and other items. Catalogue shopping is convenient and fun. A few of the many mail-order suppliers are listed below: Consult gardening magazines and local garden supply stores for others, and send away for your own collection.

UNITED STATES

Clapper's
1125 Washington Street
West Newton, MA 02165

Gardener's Eden
P.O. Box 7307
San Francisco, CA 94120-7307

Gardener's Supply
128 Intervale Road
Burlington, VT 05401

John Deere Catalog
1400 Third Avenue
Moline, IL 61265

Plow & Hearth
560 Main Street
Madison, VA 22727

Ringer
9959 Valley View Road
Eden Prairie, MN 55344-3585

Smith & Hawken
25 Corte Madera
Mill Valley, CA 94941

The Garden Book Club
250 West 57th Street
New York, NY 10107

CANADA

Dominion Seed House
115 Guelph Street
Georgetown, Ontario
L7G 4A2

Alberta Nurseries and Seeds Ltd.
Box 20
Bowden, Alberta
T0M 0K0

November 19 – November 25

YEAR 1

YEAR 2

YEAR 3

Zen Gardens

SIT QUIETLY. BREATHE IN SLOWLY. EXHALE. MEDITATE on the possibilities of a Zen garden. Envision soothing ripples and waves in the sand or gravel, or the stillness and purity of a snow-covered winter garden.

A Japanese garden represents in miniature the elements of the larger world. A single rock calls to mind a mountain; dwarf evergreens, a forest. Flagstone step-paths, wooden gates, and pebble ponds are common structures; azaleas, ferns, boxwood hedges, and flowering cherry are favorite plants.

Strategically placed ornaments will enhance the garden's theme. A hanging lantern will illuminate a special area of the garden for evening view. A stone basin that catches rainwater and reflects the sky can be a focal point. Consider the seasons as well—in winter frozen water hanging from a bamboo spout will arrest the eye.

November 26 – December 2

YEAR 1

YEAR 2

YEAR 3

Bonsai

BONSAI-GROWING IS ONE OF THE MOST EXACTing garden arts. Masterpiece bonsai are valued for their age—the most valuable may reach 300 years of age. This longevity is the result of careful cutting and maintenance. There are two groups of bonsai—trees and grasses. Trees include pines and oaks, foliage trees (Japanese maple); fruit trees (persimmon or crabapple); and flowering trees (cherry). Grass bonsai consists of shrubs, mosses, and bamboo.

You can start your own bonsai: Buy a young evergreen, such as a five-year-old juniper, at a local nursery. Transplant it from a one-gallon container to a shallow Japanese dish, using sandy soil to achieve proper water drainage. The bonsai method is to prune the roots and branches carefully, and confine growth to a minimum. You will probably find it useful at this point to take a class in bonsai training or to read some reference books for ideas on how to proceed.

December 3 - December 9

YEAR 1

YEAR 2

YEAR 3

Holiday Decorations

PINE BOUGHS OVER THE MANTELPIECE, flames from the yule log, hot cider to drink—it's holiday season once again, and time to create holiday decorations.

- Deorate the tree with a special theme or color scheme.
- Make an evergreen wreath of balsam, fir, pine, Norway spruce, red cedar, juniper, yew, or boxwood.
- Gather pinecones for a wreath or centerpiece.
- Fashion a garland with raffia, pine, dried roses, hydrangea, and baby's breath.
- Make a dried flower tree. You will need a styrofoam cone, a thick twig, a terra-cotta pot, some plaster of Paris, and dried mosses and flowers. Adhere the twig inside the pot with plaster. Pierce the cone down onto the twig. Glue moss over cone and add layers of your favorite dried flowers.
- Place decorative and fragrant baskets full of pinecones, lavender, kitchen herbs, or potpourri around the house.
- Fill footed bowls with spicy pomanders.
- Make rosemary topiaries fastened with large red bows.
- Bend a wire hanger into a heart-shape and make a wreath of ribbons, baby's breath, and roses.
- Start herbs in small pots. Snip fresh sage, parsley, basil, and lemon verbena for decorating Christmas serving platters.
- Grapevine wreaths make lovely centerpieces, welcome door signs, or gifts, personalized with eucalyptus and holly berries.

December 10 – December 16

YEAR 1

YEAR 2

YEAR 3

Designing for Year-Round Effect

There is no reason, other than poor planning, that there cannot be something to enjoy in the garden all year round. Even in winter, weatherproof ornaments and beautifully shaped trees can provide visual interest in the garden.

When the flowers are gone and the autumn colors have faded, there can still be something to look forward to. Autumn- and winter-flowering plants (such as witch hazel), trees with colorful or interestingly patterned barks (silvery birches, aspen, snow gum, lace-bark pine), and plants with berries (holly plants especially) all add color and interest to a winter landscape.

Dramatic lighting on ice-coated tree branches or snow-blanketed shrubbery lends a whole new perspective to the garden winter. Garden ornaments and statuary will take on a new importance when the colors of spring, summer, and autumn give way to the browns, grays, and whites of winter.

December 17 - December 23

YEAR 1

YEAR 2

YEAR 3

Pomanders

A WONDERFUL HOLIDAY ACTIVITY IS MAKING spice pomanders. Many commercial versions—china balls filled with potpourri—are available at holiday time. It is easy to make your own pomanders, however, and more fun than buying them.

- Gather firm oranges, lemons, apples, and whole cloves.
- Mix powdered baking spices together:

    4 parts cinnamon

    2 parts cloves

    1 part allspice and nutmeg

    (if available, add 1 part orris root)
- Store extra in a airtight plastic bag or hermetic jar.
- Insert cloves in the fruit in a design or linear pattern, or at random.
- If you want to hang the pomander, leave a groove around the fruit for a decorative ribbon.
- Bury the pomanders in a large bowl with the spice mixture.
- Turn over mixture and pomanders week after week until they are hardened.
- Use in closets to repel moths or anywhere in the home you wish to smell of sweet spices.

December 24 - December 31

YEAR 1

YEAR 2

YEAR 3

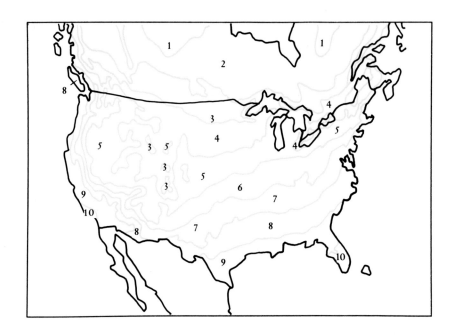

Hardiness Map

Zone 1	Below −50°F
Zone 2	−50°F to −40°F
Zone 3	−40°F to −30°F
Zone 4	−30°F to −20°F
Zone 5	−20°F to −10°F
Zone 6	−10°F to 0°F
Zone 7	0°F to 10°F
Zone 8	10°F to 20°F
Zone 9	20°F to 30°F
Zone 10	30°F to 40°F

Notes

Notes

Notes

Maria C. Gleason is a horticulturist and professional gardening consultant. Director of Secret Gardens Consultants, she specializes in city and terrace gardening and interior plantscaping. Ms. Gleason's experience also includes corporate garden design and flower arranging. A wildflower expert, she was formerly the horticulturist at the New York Botanical Garden's Shop-in-the-Garden in Manhattan's IBM building.

Walter Chandoha is a well-known writer and photographer who specializes in nature and animal subjects. His photos have appeared in hundreds of publications, and he is the author and photographer of more than twenty books.